Labouring Words

Kurtis Asha

BookLeaf Publishing

Presentation by *BookLeaf Publishing*

Web: www.bookleafpub.com

E-mail: info@bookleafpub.com

ISBN: 9789357442206

First edition 2023

*Dedicated to Sofinha Halfpint & Fredstar,
quite fond of you both.*

PREFACE

I wrote this book of limericks on a challenge, this may draw parallels with Mary Shelley's motivation to write Frankenstein but to manage your expectations, the quality and finesse of this book in comparison are leagues behind. Light years, even.

The curation of this book came at a time of growth, in that my family unit increased by 1 with the introduction of my 1st born. Which led to the theme's you'll find in this book of limericks. Based on memories of life as an expectant father up until my bouncing baby boy turning 23 months. During this time there was little that consumed my head space more than him and his mother.

The process to keep motivated was firmly rooted in the sunk-cost fallacy, paying a premium to make sure I wrote at least 18 poems, 1 for every day for the sake of money already spent. I found it worked well, especially when converting money spent to how much pizza I could have consumed with it.

I wrote limericks during breakfast, on the toilet, upside down on my bed, whilst getting my son to sleep. No location was off limits. I would like to acknowledge predictive text in facilitating my efforts.

Where will this lead? Who knows, I'll try anything once, this is my "try writing a book of poetry" for once. To parrot what I've wrote for the book description. I hope that reading this will jog your memory of moments as an expectant parent, or at the least, just make you smile. Even a wry one.

Poppy Seed

There once was a soon to be grandad
that was about to be told that he had a
grandson on the way
the words were relayed
via baby shark do-do-da-da

Banana

2

There once was a lady in her third trimester
burning stomach of lava, she festered
she had a clue
of what to do
and ate a Gaviscon smoothie for breakfast

Little Pumpkin

Our neighbour offered a favour
I'll drive you when you're in labour
knocked on for some pears
she sped down the stairs
a spot of whiplash it gave her

1cm

There once was an independent lady
turns out, she was having a baby
to partner palms bare
I am under your care
with haste, checked into hospital ably

2cm

There once was a couple in the labour room
who had food prepared and download Splatoon
pain in showers
for 37 hours
and not a game played or a crumb consumed

3cm

There were 6 student nurses with greetings
all arranged single file for meeting
a soon to be mother that's at
8 inches dilation that's fact
rather than caring to her needing's

4cm

There once was a nurse with magical hands
her back message was not in the plans
dad tried to copy
results were sloppy
looked dead in the eye, you're not meeting
demand

5cm

There once was a lady in labour
from pain we need to save her
cannister a new
gas and air in lieu
but the gauge was zero, amateur

6cm

Push when you think it feels right
wrong instruction, details a little light
as natural as it felt
she pushed passed her belt
to find no baby, just a little shite

7cm

There once was a lady in and out of pain
on the road to delivery in the slow lane
"they're not listening to me
trying my best for baby"
in the end and epidural was not deigned

8cm

There once was lady on pethidine
whose contractions were getting lean
a nurse then claimed
no fault for maim
and was titled a ducking butter bean

9cm

Between contractions and throes of pain
Bite a stick to keep you sane
options null
so, dads' hair she pulls
his follicles now removed from brain

10cm

13

There once was a baby expected
by uterus was protected
with just a tilt
blood was spilt
and mum and baby connected

Mercury

There once was a man who cried rarely
found himself in theatre, how dare he
umbilical cut
without so much as a tut
became a blubbering mess, a cry-baby

There once was a new born in muslin
tired new mum, face blank, a la Moomin
dad with headache
go now medicate
reflect on the moment and get clued in

Venus

There once was a new born with low weight
a bundle of cuddle, our little "po-tate"
blood from heel
his little squeal
1 pound was missed the nurse I'll berate

Post-natal ward is a place of drudge
wear bedside manners not worth a smudge
a sole nurse then whispered, if you would
new mother, listen here, you're doing good
at least there's one ward angel I misjudged

Earth

There was a new born to rollover quick
Who loved balls and rattles and all that shtick
He barely kicked
And rarely flipped
But daily downward dog like a hinged
matchstick

There once was a toddler who growled
and cry and sometimes howled
what calmed him down
was a book we found
a book called "wow said the owl"

He's as sharp as they come my son
and now he's learning shapes for fun
give me a shape if you dare
expecting a square
so, he drew a dodecagon

Mars

I had little expectations of being a parent
expect of course the genes that are inherent
what I did not expect
and not by choice select
my mouth catching babies drool transparent

There was a new father who intently
pushed his baby on the swings gently
baby was bored and sighed
mum pushed him high
now looky-here baby chuckles loudly

Jupiter

There once was a baby that's it
being moved naked to fit
a new nappy that's clean
but poo flew between
so, daddy though to catch it

My son is tactical with his poos
and knows to go when he's moved
for instance, last night
the mood did strike
at bath time he stood, let rip and loose

Saturn

There once was a toddler who liked to seethe
the mounted rage made it hard to breathe
his hands in fists
his body in twists
all because we asked to brush his teeth

My son loves broccoli with all his heart
if it's not on the menu he'd rather dart
over chocolate and cream
or a shot of morphine
if broccoli's not present he'd fall apart

Uranus

My toddler looked at me and then at my chest
Daddy he said, "where are your breasts"
he looked bemused
really confused
looked at my nipples, spiders he guessed

Our young boy has cottoned on
the ideal son, our eidolon
we get home he says
with swagger and sways
where's "The Mummy" gone

Neptune

There was a toddler with two train sets
he had many toys as well as two pets
a whale that glows
a bike that folds
but he wants to play "wobble cups" as a duet

There once was a small boy, a little whisper
rapt by the milky way, our little mr
his words were new
from lips they flew
recalled the planets and the "soul systah"